HUSH

Don't Say Anything
to God

HUSH

Don't Say Anything to God

Passionate Poems
of Rumi

by
SHAHRAM SHIVA

JAIN PUBLISHING COMPANY
FREMONT, CALIFORNIA

Library of Congress Cataloging-in-Publication Data

Ja lāl al–Dīn Rūmī, Maulana, 1207–1273.
   [Dīvān–i Shams–i Tabrīzī. English. Selections]
   Hush, don't say anything to God : passionate poems of Rumi / by
Shahram Shiva.
      p. cm.
     ISBN 0-87573-084-1 (pbk. : alk. paper)
     I. Shiva, Sharam.   II. Title.
   PK6481.D6E5 1999 c
   891'.5511– –dc21

                             99–31638
                                 CIP

Cover & Book Design: Leslie Waltzer

Shahram Shiva's Web Site
www.rumi.net

Jain Publishing Company's Web Site
www.jainpub.com

*Dedicated to the little known
Persian aspect of Lord Shiva.*

He smiled like a rose in full bloom,
    he said, come into the heart of fire.
There you will see
    what you thought was a flame,
    is only jasmine.
What you thought was heat,
    is only a leaf on a tree.
What you thought was a blinding glow,
    is only a bed of tulips,
    walk right in,
    and, hush, don't say anything.
Flames turned into a talking rose,
    the heat cradled me in its gentle arms,
    it said, except of the kindness,
    and generosity of the Beloved,
    don't say anything to God.

ACKNOWLEDGMENTS

A thousand hearts of gratitude to the following:
- Khanum Naz Tadayyon Shiva
- Gurumayi Chidvilasananda
- Erica Bilder for her generosity
- Edo & Alex Born for their generosity
- Edo Born for the whirling demonstration photography
- Mukesh Jain

and

Michael Harrison, Akal Dev Sharonne, John Ragusa and Linda Worster for their feedback on the manuscript.

also

Qalbi, Deepak Chopra, Margo Anand, Brian Keane, Omar Faruk Tekbilek, Jonathan Star, Robin Becker, Rich Goodhart, Randy Crafton, Jorge Alfano, John Funkhouser, Eric Edberg, Bruce Detrick, R.A. Fish, Jesika Gastongvay, Charlotte Pharr, Keve Wilson, Cybele Paschke, Bahram Tadayyon, Reza Namazi, Alan & Merilyn Bergman, Ricki & Miles, Roger Waters, The Abode of the Message, New York Open Center, Sufi Books, and Joey Whittaker,.

The preparation of the manuscript of this book was made possible in part through generous grants from Edo & Alex Born and Erica Bilder.

CONTENTS

Like the way a garden burns
  in a hundred shades of orange in the fall,
  a Lover's heart shrivels for a sense of the Beloved's touch.
  Now the face of that charred garden
  is my field of flowers.
                                        —RUMI

Rumi is now the best read poet in America. Every time I hear this state-
ment I get a warm feeling in my heart. I began translating Rumi in 1988,
and performing his poetry in 1990. In all of these years I never thought
that he would become so popular in the West, in such a short time.
Rumi-I am constantly reminded-is a miracle. Everything about him is
absolute magic, from the story of his life, to his super-human ability of
remaining in constant touch with the flow of intense creative energy for
more than two decades. In addition, he inspired the *Mevlevi Order* of The
Whirling Dervishes, who continue his passion for whirling today, and
tour the world.

Rumi was born on the Eastern shores of the Persian Empire in 1207,
and finally settled in the town of Konya, in what is now Turkey. His life
story reads like a fairy tale. A genius theologian, a pillar of Islam, a brilliant
sober scholar, meets a wandering wild darvish by the name of Shams
of Tabriz, and almost overnight is transformed into an enraptured lover
of God. It seems that the universe brought these two opposing characters
together to remind us for eternity that it is never what you expect when
it comes to mysticism. It is impossible to know where your next inspi-
ration may come from, or who will become the conduit for your trans-
formation. For Rumi the life of mystics is a "gathering of lovers, where
there is no high or low, smart or ignorant, no proper schooling
required." Rumi and his spiritual friend Shams left an undying legacy of
the way-of-the-heart triumphing over intellect and logic.

I often wonder about the similarities between the lives of Jesus and Rumi, specifically the issue of Sham's disappearance. Rumi wouldn't have become who he is today had it not been for Shams disappearing on him. Shams leaving Rumi can be likened to Jesus dying on the cross. Jesus willingly put himself on the cross for the salvation of humanity (see poem *Secrets of the Death of Lovers*), and Shams volunteered to die (no mortal force could have really killed that wild man of Tabriz, who was known for his amazing spiritual powers) for Rumi to become who he is today. After Shams died, Rumi plunged himself into poetry and 25 years and some 70,000 verses later he made his mark on the world as the greatest mystical poet of any age (even though he never did consider himself a professional poet). No wonder he named his first collection of poems Divan-e Shams-e Tabrizi (the collective poems of Shams of Tabriz). Could he have become a poet had it not been for Shams? All evidence points to the contrary. (See *Dreams and Initiations* in the back of this book for further analysis of Shams and Rumi's relationship.)

Some years ago Pir Vilayat Inayat Khan asked me if I thought it was Shams that had come through Rumi in all those thousands of poems. I replied that I thought Rumi became a vessel for Shams' creative energy. But now that I have been able to spend more time attuning to Rumi, I have come to a different conclusion. I think that for anyone with a good knowledge of Persian and some understanding of the way-of-the-heart, it would become clear that the character and personality of Rumi are alive and well through every verse. These are indeed words of Rumi, colored and perfumed with every particle of his being. The *Divan* is teeming with his charm and his charisma. The *Divan* is the expression of a man brilliant in the way of the sciences, the Koranic studies and the way of a true darvish, or as Rumi calls it, *marde khodaa* (man of God). Rumi was just such a man. All of these reveals Rumi inspired by Shams and fueled by God's highest level of divine indoctrination.

This selection of quatrains and odes has been in the making since 1994. The theme is Passion. These are some of my favorite poems of Rumi and they deal in one way or another with Love and its many facets. They are about the joy of the lover and the beloved embracing, the pain of separation, the unnecessary childish games that make no sense at all but are part of the everyday fabric of being in love, the anguish, the invisible bloodshed, the escapes, the returns, the sacrifices, the humility, the acceptance, the teachings, the hypocrisy, the hide and seek, the secret meetings, the gut-wrenching pain and the willingness to die for ones loved one. Having been in love may be a prerequisite to appreciate this selection. For those of you new to Rumi, I have two words, watch out! You may be deeply moved by exploring this side of him.

I believe some notes on the poems are in order. As many of you know Rumi spoke poetry, he did not just sit down and write words on paper. Poetry in perfect rhyme and meter poured out of him as he whirled for hours on end, or as he fell into various states of ecstasy and rapture. There is movement in every verse of Rumi. There is music, rhythm and breath in most of his poems in Persian. I have often said that these poems are autobiographical, he uttered the words as he experienced the emotions. His creative expression is as far away from an intellectual process as you can imagine. In my work as a translator I try to bring out some of these nuances. I try to pay a special attention to Rumi as a Persian mystic, and to the origin and the method of the creation of these timeless, sublime and always magical words.

These are some of my most cherished poems of Rumi, and two in particular are quite famous in Persian culture. In fact, the first verse of the poem *Intellect Lost* is a proverb, and the section about the Sheikh wandering the streets at night in I *Crave to Hear You Say*, is an example of what many Persians might recite under their lips as they conduct their daily chores. But my favorite poem is *Sailing Toward Tabriz*. The first time that I translated this poem, the part about the anchor of his soul inhibiting him from moving forward caused me to weep uncontrollably for more than an hour. The section about the Beloved running a head-boiling shop refers to the Persian mystical term *sar sepordan* (to give one's head in trust). When a master accepts a disciple it is said that the disciple gives his head (his being) in trust to the master. One can assume that a master can then have a collection of many heads, hence the reference to him as a head seller. My favorite verse, however, is the first line from *I Have Come to Shine*. After reading it all I wanted to say to Rumi was "please do."

Those of you who have read my 1992 book with Jonathan Star *A Garden Beyond Paradise*, may find some of the quatrains reappearing in this book with minor adjustments. These are quatrains that I consider to be classics, and since the book has been out of print for so long, I decided to offer them again to new readers. Also I translated the poem *Lover Me* in 1990, and a rendition of it appeared in *A Garden Beyond Paradise*. (This poem is one of Rumi's most famous as well and the Persian classical singer Shahram Nazeri has sung a magnificent version of it.) The Persian of *Lover Me* is a special poem (these four opening words set the rhythm for the entire poem in Persian: *yaar maraa, ghaar maraa*; lover for me, cave for me), it is one of Rumi's most rhythmical and minimal poems. I always wondered about the possibility of a new English rendition that would do justice to the original ultra-minimal version. It wasn't until I came across the lyrics of *Summer Me, Winter Me* by Alan & Marilyn Bergman, sung by the late Sylvia Syms, that I realized the possibility of a style that could bring the feeling of the Persian to the English speaking readers. This rendition of *Lover Me* is inspired by their lyrics.

Most of these poems appear in English for the first time. I have also included a section on whirling in this book. Whirling was such an important part of Rumi's life and in my experience, many of you want to start turning like the planets. So give that section of the book a whirl, as they say, and after you have become comfortable with the notion of perpetual turning, you may want to recite your favorite verses of Rumi out loud while whirling, the way Rumi did himself.

May the wisdom of Shams continually inspire us and may his compassion be a guiding light on our path to unity.

In peace,

Shahram Shiva
September 23, 1998

QUATRAINS

To Love is to reach God.
Never will a Lover's chest
    feel any sorrow.
Never will a Lover's robe
    be touched by mortals.
Never will a Lover's body
    be found buried in the earth.
To Love is to reach God.

To heal the burning of your sorrow,
    I seek a flame.
To gather the dust of your door,
    I seek the palms of my hands.
To deal with you hiding behind your holiness,
    I seek a good time instead.

It is your turn now,
    you waited, you were patient.
    The time has come,
    for us to polish you.
    We will transform your inner pearl
    into a house of fire.
You're a gold mine.
    Did you know that,
    hidden in the dirt of the earth?
It is your turn now,
    to be placed in fire.
    Let us cremate your impurities.

How do we do it?
I am not sure sometimes.
I am head strong,
    head drunk and
    at times a little foolish.
He is sensitive,
    has no patience and
    gets bored very easily.
The only reason we are still together,
    is that
    God is the one running our messages.

The Lovers
    will drink wine night and day.
They will drink until they can
    tear away the veils of intellect and
    melt away the layers of shame
    and modesty.
When in Love,
    body, mind, heart and soul
    don't even exist.
    Become this,
    fall in Love,
    and you will not be separated again.

Love rests on no foundation.
  It is an endless ocean,
  with no beginning or end.
Imagine,
  a suspended ocean,
  riding on a cushion of ancient secrets.
All souls have drowned in it,
  and now dwell there.
One drop of that ocean is hope,
  and the rest is fear.

Look around you.
If you see happiness,
    it is of Love's doing.
If joy could talk,
    this is what She would say,
    "it was Love who gave birth to me."
As for myself,
    the only mother I know is Love.
Long ago, since the beginning of time,
    it was Love who gave birth to me.
A hundred blessings to my true mother.

Love is the one constant in the universe.
Love is from the infinite and
    will be until eternity.
The seeker of Love
    is free from the carousel
    ride of the soul.
When the apocalypse comes,
any heart that is not in Love
will fail the test.

The Lover is not a Moslem,
    be sure of that.
Since in the religion of Love,
    there is no blasphemy or faith.
When in Love,
    body, mind, heart and soul
    don't even exist.
    Become this,
    fall in Love,
    you will not be separated again.

We are all powerless by Love's game.
How can you expect us
   to behave and act modest?
How can you expect us
   to stay at home, like good little boys?
How can you expect us
   to enjoy being chained like mad men?
Oh, my Beloved, you will find us every night,
   on your street,
      with our eyes glued to your window,
      waiting for a glimpse of your radiant face.

Your Love will turn a monastery
    into a tavern.
Your Love will cause a bazaar of idols to
    burst into flames.
The hands of your sorrow, like thieves,
    will find a way through all the obstacles
    and grab us in this world and the next.

This world is no match for your Love.
Being away from you
     is death aiming to take my soul away.
My heart, so precious,
     I won't trade for a hundred thousand souls.
     Your one smile takes it for free.

Your Love is the source of passion
    for all the Love there is.
It burns my soul, night and day.
Don't look for the ashes,
    you won't find any,
    they are all inside of me,
    layers upon layers,
    all inside of me.
Even a sea of passions and seductions
    could not wash these ashes away.
Wait until I am dead,
    if they open me up, you will find
    a thousand eyes,
    staring you in the face.

I am an atom;
>   you are like the countenance
>   of the Sun for me.
I am a patient of Love
>   you are like medicine for me.
Without wings, without feathers,
>   I fly about looking for you.
I have become a rose petal
>   and you are like the wind for me.
Take me for a ride.

I said, meet me in the garden.
    You know the one—
    it is called *Smiling Spring*.
There are nightingales chirping away,
    wine and candle lights,
    and companions as soft as
    pomegranate blossoms.
You think this all would sound so perfect!
    But without you by my side,
    what use is the *Smiling Spring*?
 And when you are with me,
    what use are pomegranate blossoms?

Look what you've done to me;
    I am disheveled, bewildered, confused.
    Now please take my hand.
I am wandering about,
    in awe and amazement of you.
    Take my hand.
Everyone
    has someone to care for them.
But look at me: I have no one.
    Take my hand.

My face is that of autumn,
    yours that of spring.
My face is like a thorn and
    yours like a rose.
Unless these two come together,
    a flower cannot be formed.
In the first glance, rose and thorns
    don't look anything alike.
But look at them through my eyes,
    and you will laugh at this
    secret garden of joy.

I am dazed of the thought of you,
    night and day.
I will place my head at your feet,
    night and day.
Day and night, I will go mad for you.
    Without you,
    how can I pass these nights and days?
In the path of Love,
    a lover is asked to give away
    his heart and his soul.
    I offer my heart and soul
    night and day.

Reach for the bite
　　that doesn't fit in your mouth.
Reach for the knowledge
　　that doesn't fit in your intellect.
There is a secret in the heart of the people of
God.
　　Reach for that secret
　　that even Gabriel doesn't know.

Tonight
    is the night.
It's the creation of that land of eternity.
It's not an ordinary night,
    it's a wedding of those who seek God.
Tonight, the bride and groom
    speak in one tongue.
Tonight, the bridal chamber
    is looking particularly well.

Do you know what you are?
    You are a manuscript of a divine letter.
    You are a mirror reflecting a noble face.
This universe is not outside of you.
    Look inside yourself;
    everything that you want,
    you are already that.

You think of yourself
    as a citizen of the universe.
You think you belong
    to this world of dust and matter.
Out of this dust
    you have created a personal image,
    and have forgotten
    about the essence of your true origin.

Last night,
I saw the realm of joy and pleasure.
    There I melted like salt;
    no religion, no blasphemy,
    no conviction or uncertainty remained.
In the middle of my heart,
    a star appeared,
    and the seven heavens were lost
    in its brilliance.

Oh my heart,
    don't become discouraged
    so easily.
    Have faith.
In the hidden world,
    there are many mysteries,
    many wonders.
Even if the whole planet
    threatens you with your life.
    don't let go of the Beloved's robe
    for even a breath.

When we talk about the witness in our verse,
 we talk about you.
A pure heart and a noble demeanor
 cannot compete with your radiant face.
They will ask you
 what you have produced.
Say to them,
 except for Love,
 what else can a Lover produce?

My head is bursting
    with the joy of the unknown.
My heart is expanding a thousand fold.
Every cell,
    taking wings,
    flies about the world.
All seek separately
    the many faces of my Beloved.

The Lover is ever drunk with Love.
  He is mad,
  she is free.
  He sings with delight,
  she dances with ecstasy.
Caught by our own thoughts,
  we worry about everything.
But once we get drunk on that Love
  whatever will be, will be.

If you die, the Lord will give you another life.
    This is the truth of living;
    it is meant to be transitory,
    not everlasting.
Love
    is the life-giving nectar of immortality;
    it is what we call the *water of life*.
Come into this water,
    walk right in,
    and see that every drop,
    is an ocean all on its own.

There is a candle in your heart,
    ready to be kindled.
There is a void in your soul,
    ready to be filled.
You feel it, don't you?
You feel the separation
    from the Beloved.
Invite Him to fill you up,
    embrace the fire.
Remind those who tell you otherwise that
    Love
    comes to you of its own accord,
    and the yearning for it
    cannot be learned in any school.

Love came,
and became like blood in my body.
It rushed through my veins and
encircled my heart.
Everywhere I looked,
I saw one thing.
The Beloved's name written
on my limbs,
on my left palm,
on my forehead,
on the back of my neck,
on my right big toe . . .
Oh, my friend,
all that you see of me
is just a shell,
and the rest belongs to the Beloved.

Here is my dilemma.
Please help me understand.
Your Love is a healer,
    your Love is a wise master,
    your Love is radiant,
    your Love is delicate and
    is soft in its essence.
I would gladly endure all this fire,
    all this yearning,
    all this burning,
    for your Love,
But if your Love is so pleasant,
    why does it hurt so much?

My body can exist
    on your Love alone.
    Why do I need this soul?
Your Love,
    so delicate,
    so sweet,
    what is it made of?
It permeates my inside,
    it envelops my outside.
Tell me the truth;
    is this your Love,
    or is this the glance of
    Shams of Tabriz
    that's enamoring my soul?

This is a gathering of Lovers.
In this gathering
    there is no high, no low,
    no smart, no ignorant,
    no special assembly,
    no grand discourse,
    no proper schooling required.
    There is no master,
    no disciple.
This gathering is more like a drunken party,
    full of tricksters, fools,
    mad men and mad women.
This is a gathering of Lovers.

I am in Love!
I am in Love with him.
  All this advise—
  what's the use?
I have drunk poison.
  All this sugar
  what's the use?
You say hurry,
  tie up his feet.
But its my heart that's gone crazy,
  all this rope
  around my feet—
  what's the use?

Last night,
    my Lover came.
    He must have been in a kind mood
    to finally show up.
I asked the night
    not to reveal my secret.
Night said,
    who do you think you're fooling?
    You own the Sun,
    you own the daylight.
    Can I even appear in the morning
    to tell anyone about this?

Last night
   my Lover came.
   He was drunk,
   and began caressing my hair.
My face was picking tulips from his face.
I said,
   you don't have to embrace me so hard.
   Don't worry, I am not going anywhere.
   From the time my face was created,
   it never turned away from the ka'ba
   of your face.

Last night,
    I ran my name through mud
    a thousand times.
I was pulling and grabbing
    on that hypocrite's robe.
From the joy and excitement of our union,
    our hearts melted into one.
As for my reputation and my name,
    I smashed it on a rock
    like a piece of glass.

Love is best when mixed with anguish.
In our town,
    we won't call you a Lover
    if you escape the pain.
Look for Love in this way,
    welcome it to your soul,
    and watch your spirit fly away in ecstasy.

I am drumming,
I am drumming,
I am drumming
    for my Love's ever nearing union.
They say get a life.
    What is all this drumming?
I swear to that Love,
    the day that I stop drumming,
    is the day that I will stop living.

There is a certain Love
    that is formed out of the
    elixir of the East.
There is a certain cloud,
    impregnated with a
    thousand lightnings.
There is my body,
    in it an ocean formed of his glory,
    all the creation,
    all the universes,
    all the galaxies,
    are lost in it.

I am your servant,
I am your servant,
I am the servant
    of your lips full of laughter.
You are the source of life.
You are the elixir of immortality.
They ask, aren't you worried about death?
How can I be?
    When I have become immortal, like Khezr
    because of you.

Go ahead: ask me!
Ask me about Love,
 and I will tell you the essence
 of madness.
Ask me of an intellect gone mad,
 and I will show you a soul
 departed for good.
Ask me of a hundred calamities,
 of a hundred life transformations.
Ask me of a hundred deserts engulfed in fire.
Ask me of a hundred oceans red with blood.

This is what I see.
The world is green,
    and everywhere there is a garden.
I see your face,
    luminous like a rose,
    I see you happy,
    you are laughing.
Everywhere there is a gem,
    inflamed from the Beloved's mine.
Everywhere there is a soul,
    connected to another soul.

I saw sorrow
    holding a cup of pain.
I said, hey sorrow,
    sorry to see you this way.
    What's troubling you?
    What's with the cup?
Sorrow said,
    what else can I do?
    All this Joy that you have brought
    to the world
    has killed my business completely.

Your Love
    has ravished my heart and
    enraptured my soul.
For the killing of my impurities,
    you have used every magic
    you could summon.
I can say this to you now.
In offering
    ALL of your Love to my heart.
You are not aware,
    how many blasphemous deeds
    you have done.
    How many laws your have broken.

Neither I am me,
    nor you are you,
    nor you are me.
Also, I am me,
    you are you
    and you are me.
We have become one
    in such a way,
That I am confused whether
    I am you,
    or you are me.

You kiss the lips of everyone
   who asks for your sweetness.
When it is my turn,
   you turn your face
   and come up with excuses.
You pardon everyone's crime
   without even a reason.
But when it is my crime,
   you tag some more wrongdoings
   and give it arms and legs.

You think you are alive
    because you breathe air?
    Shame on you,
    that you are alive in such a limited way.
Don't be without Love,
    so you won't feel dead.
Die in Love
    and stay alive forever.

Do you know
    what this night really is about?
Listen, Oh wise one.
But first get every stranger
    out of this gathering.
Tonight is very special,
    because I am housemate with the moon.
    I am drunk.
    Moon is in Love,
    and the night has gone completely mad.

There is a hidden treasure
    deep within the Earth.
    It is covered from the infidels and
    people of faith alike.
I have seen this treasure,
    and it is
    Love.
The ancient treasure that the legends
    are made of,
    is Love.
When I saw that,
    I tore off my garments.
I will not be covered again,
    until Love is uncovered.

I wish I could give you a taste of
    the burning fire of Love.
There is a fire
    blazing inside of me.
    If I cry about it, or if I don't,
    the fire is at work,
    night and day.
People make clothing to cover their intellect,
    but the heart of Lovers
    is a shroud,
    inflamed in golden hues of his Love.

I swallowed
    some of the Beloved's sweet wine,
    and now I am ill.
    My body aches,
    my fever is high.
They called in the Doctor and he said,
    drink this tea!
    Ok, time to drink this tea.
Take these pills!
    Ok, time to take these pills.
The Doctor said,
    get rid of the sweet wine of his lips!
    Ok, time to get rid of the doctor.

Stop!
Stop right there!
You have the reached
    the fortress of the heart.
Yes, the voice
    is coming from inside you.
A new stage in your meditation
    has been reached.
From this point on
    you will see amazing wonders.
    You will see a moon
    which is always full.
    You will see breasts of a lioness
    abundant with milk.
All inside of you.
    All inside of you.
Go ahead, taste that milk.
    You are a lion's cub.
    Drink your fill.

I have created you out of flames,
and am now placing you into fire.
You are with me,
    always,
      but not aware of me
      all the time.
I am a sorcerer,
    and have put a spell on you.
      Now try to get away.

Tonight
    I am your guest.
    Don't go to sleep.
You are my heart and my soul.
    Don't go to sleep.
When your face came through that door,
    this night became a holy night.
    Oh, the king of those who seek Love.
    Oh, the cypress covering
    two hundred orchards.
    Oh, the garden of the *Smiling Spring*.
    Oh, the calming of the heart
    of the drunkards.
    Don't go to sleep.
Without you the two worlds
    are nothing but a prison.
    Alas, don't go to sleep.

Tonight
is the night
when the secrets
will be revealed.
Don't go back to sleep.
Think of yourself as Jupiter
and turn around the moon.
Thank God that others are fast asleep,
because the creator and I have
much work to do tonight.

A true Lover has
    no fear of the path.
Be sure of that.
Those in Love walk with the
    ancient one.
Know this,
    Love and the Lover are one.
Oh the light in my eyes,
    the generosity that befalls you
    is from Shams alone.

I am so drunk
I have lost the way in
     and the way out.
I have lost the earth, the moon, and the sky.
Don't put another cup of wine in my hand,
     pour it in my mouth,
          for I have lost the way to my mouth.

Oh Beloved,
    take me.
    Liberate my soul.
    Fill me with your love and
    release me from the two worlds.
If I set my heart on anything but you
    let fire burn me from inside.
Oh Beloved,
    take away what I want.
    Take away what I do.
    Take away what I need.
    Take away everything
    that takes me from you.

By day I praised you
    and never knew it.
By night I stayed with you
    and never knew it.
I always thought that
    I was me—but no,
    I was you
    and never knew it.

ODES

⚜

LOVE SAID TO ME

I worship the moon.
    Tell me of the soft glow of a
    candle light
    and the sweetness of my moon.
Don't talk about sorrow,
    tell me of the treasure,
    hidden if it is to you,
    then just remain silent.
Last night
    I lost my grip on reality
    and welcomed insanity.
    Love
    saw me and said,
    I showed up.
    Wipe you face
    and be silent.
I said, O Love
    I am frightened,
    but it's not you.
    Love said to me,
    there is nothing that is not me.
    Just be silent.
I will whisper secrets in your ear
    just nod yes
    and be silent.
A soul moon
    appeared in the path of my heart.
    How precious is this journey.

I said, O Love
    what kind of moon is this?
    Love said to me,
    this is not for you to question.
    Just be silent.
I said, O Love
    what kind of face is this,
    angelic, or human?
    Love said to me,
    this is beyond anything that you know.
    Be silent.
I said, please reveal this to me
    I am dying in anticipation.
    Love said to me,
    that is where I want you,
    always on the edge,
    be silent.
You dwell in this hall of
    images and illusions,
    leave this house now
    and be silent.
I said, O Love,
    tell me this,
    does the Lord know you are
    treating me this way?
    Love said to me,
    yes He does, just
    be totally, totally silent.

BIRD OF HEAVENS

Last night
my heart disappeared.
    I think it was at the tavern.
    I was gone, wasted,
      my heart got detached and left me
      somewhere far far away.
He knew it was time to go.
Last night
I finally set my intellect free,
    severed the dependence.
    When my heart saw that,
    he took wings and flew.
He didn't go to another tavern,
    nor did he go to the market place.
He took flight to the solitude of the Lord.
Don't look for him at the
house of my friend Zarkub,
    or in the bazaar of exotic birds.
    My heart is a bird of heavens,
    and has gone to the heavens.
My heart is a white falcon worthy of the king's,
    and has gone to the king of kings.

SAILING TOWARD TABRIZ

Look what I have found.
    I found Shams, I found a cup
    In its core I found
    the spring of the Sun.
What radiance, what glow,
    his chest is beaming
    with such light
    the eyes can not endure.
    Thank the lord,
    I've found such a sweetheart.
I found the locks of his hair,
    I found myself.
    My heart in wonder!
    Think of it this way,
    I went to the core of
    the fragrant musk,
    I found an amber.
They may ask you to reveal
    what you found,
    say,
    I found
    in the goblet,
    teeming with the finest ruby red,
    a Lover, a youth, a drunkard
    all in one.

If they don't believe you
    grasp hold of their throat,
    drag them on the ground,
    rub dirt on their faces,
    say, I found
    I found, a non-believer.
In the midst of the locks of his hair,
    I found fire.
    I say this to you
    maybe then you will understand,
    in the core of amber and musk
    I found a hot coal.
The Beloved breaks open a large ruby
    as an offering to that
    mine of rubies.
    I say this to you
    only in the core of the Sun,
    there is such mine of such radiance.
He owns a shop in the bazaar of head boilers,
    all the heads and hearts are with him.
    I went shopping in such a store,
    there were heads everywhere.
    I looked and I looked.
    I found one head.
    I found what I needed.
I became curious about heads,
    I came home,
    looked in my own head,

I saw it was full of his Love.
Then and only then,
I found the vision of
the secret of my search.
I saw then
that my searches where in vain.
I searched in the line of the
mighty warriors,
I met their king, but then I left.
I searched for a bull in
the constellation of Taurus,
found a donkey instead,
so I left.
Finally, in the place of no heritage,
in the constellation of no name,
I found the one,
the mighty bull of a man.
What more can I tell you,
my friend,
I sailed toward Tabriz, many many times,
but did not move.
I looked, guess what I found?
In my soul-boat,
I found an anchor
fastened deep in the ground.

IT IS YOUR TURN NOW

Go and rest your head on the pillow.
    Let me be by myself,
    leave me, leave this drunk,
    creature of the night,
    powerless by Love's game.
This is me, waves upon waves of rapture,
    night and day alone,
    come, forgive me if you can,
    or just go, and don't turn back.
Run away from me,
    so you won't fall into the same pain,
    avoid this path if you can,
    choose one a little healthier,
    there is only pain here.
This is me, face wet with tears,
    sitting in the corner of the
    house of sorrow.
    Sometimes I think,
    in the water of my face,
    one can place
    a hundred water mills.
The Beloved kills with no remorse,
    he has a heart of stone.
    No one can complain,
    no one can ask for blood money.

The king of the beautiful faces
    has no need to bestow his kindness
    upon you.
    O the ashen face Lover,
    have patience,
    you show kindness.
This pain is worse than death,
    it has no remedy,
    so how can I ask the Beloved to
    take it away.
Last night in a dream,
    in the side street of Love,
    I saw a Pir, he gestured to me
    with his hand
    to come near.
He said, there is a dragon on the path,
    and Love is like a shiny emerald,
with the radiance and purity of this emerald,
    you can defeat the dragon.
Leave me now, I have gone beyond myself,
    I am not all here,
    it is your turn now to greaten your gift.
Read the history of the sages,
    awaken yourself to the
    wisdom of the ages.

INTELLECT LOST

I have lost my intellect to wine,
    you have lost yours to madness,
    who then, will take us home?
I have told you a hundred times
    to drink a little less.
    Can you find a person
    still on his feet in this town?
    one worse than the other,
    drunk out of their minds.
O dear one,
    come to the tavern of the ruins,
    so you can see what real pleasure is like.
What pleasure can there be for the soul,
    without the talk of the Beloved.
In every corner a drunkard,
    and there is *saaghi*, with her kingly cup.
You are from the ruins,
    you are one with the ruins,
    wine is what you earn,
    wine is what you spend
    and of this to the sober ones,
    don't utter a word.
O the harp playing gypsy,
    who is drunker—you or I?
Outside of the house, I see a drunken man,
    in his every glance
    a hundred flower gardens.

Like a boat without an anchor,
    he sways from side to side.
    A drunkard,
    although a hundred wise men
    have died of his envy.
I said, where are you from?
He smiled and said, O dearer than my life,
    partly from the land of Turks,
    partly from *Forghan*,
    partly of water and mud,
    partly of soul and heart,
    partly from the seashore,
    and the rest,
    precious drops of pearls.
I said, please be kind to me,
    I am one of your own.
He said, to me friend and stranger are one,
    I have neither a heart nor a mind,
    I dwell in the house of the wine
    I have a chest full of words,
    which ones to say, which ones to keep.
Such a good drunk,
    can he be less than a piece of wood?
    Remember that famous wooden pillar
    that wept for her lost Beloved.
O Shams, how can you escape the public,
    now that you have turned these people
    inside out?

I'VE GOT YOU NOW

My face free of sorrow,
    my mouth full of wine,
    my clothes torn off my body.
    Look what you've done to me now.
He says, that's what I do.
    I tear away the layers.
    I melt the shame.
    I reveal the unrevealed.
He moves too fast.
    One breath, he is outside the window.
    Next breath, he is inside my shirt.
I can't think clear,
    my mind is not here,
    he is all I see.
    NOW!
    There is new life in me.
The seven heavens cannot contain him,
    but he is here,
    moving up my shirt.
    Pop, one button here.
    Pop, one button there.
This lion of God
    watches over me,
    I sing as he roars.

He says, I've got you now.
    I gave you life,
    I created you,
    I do what I want now.
I am your harp,
    play me easy,
    play me hard, or
    don't touch my strings at all.
You know!
    I think,
    I've got YOU now.
Before I met you,
    I had only one heart,
    I had only one body,
    I was only being.
But look at me now,
    I've got you now.

I CRAVE TO HEAR YOU SAY

I crave the orchards and the flower fields,
   Oh Beloved, reveal your face to me.
I crave loads upon loads of sweetness,
   Oh Beloved, open up your lips for me.
I crave the face of the radiant Sun,
   Oh the Sun of Tabriz, melt the clouds,
   stop the rain, let me bathe in your beauty.
I crave to hear you say,
   stop teasing me with these words.
I crave to hear you say,
   the king is not in tonight, go home.
I crave to hear you say,
   say anything.
I am a white whale,
   cannot be contained in this
   stream called life.
   I crave the Sea of Oman.
I crave the healing visitation of Joseph,
   I am Jacob, weeping endlessly.
I crave to travel the mountains on bare foot,
   fly over the deserts,
   can not stay here any longer.
   When you left me,
   they changed the town's name to prison.

My heart is darkened by these fickle,
    spineless friends.
    I crave the lion of God,
    I crave Rostam, the mighty warrior.
I crave the burning bush, Mount Sinai.
    I crave Moses, son of Amran,
    I have lost tolerance for this wicked pharaoh
    called life.
I crave the gathering of drunkards,
    smashing the barrels of wine,
    screaming from the top of my lungs.
    Let the ceaseless nagging of the people
    pass me by.
I crave to sing like a nightingale,
    but only you have the key to my lips,
    locked by the envy of the people.
Last night, a sheikh was
    wandering around town,
    holding a lantern,
    looking here and there.
    I heard him say,
    I have no more tolerance
    for these demons,
    I crave, I crave a human being.
I said, there is none left Sir
    believe me, I have looked.
    He said, I crave the one,
    he who can not be found.

Although I call nothing my own,
    you think any small jewel can excite me?
    I crave that mountain of rare carnelians.
Hidden from view, the light in everyone's eyes,
    his craft is revealed,
    I crave the hidden craftsman.
A cup of wine in one hand,
    zolf of my Lover in the other,
    I crave to whirl,
    an unforgettable whirl around the
    town square.
Listen to the *robaab*, can you hear what it says?
    It says, this waiting is worse than death.
    I crave the handling, the plucking fingers
    of Osman the drunk.
I also am a *robaab*, a *robaab* of Love.
    I crave the touch of my
    compassionate Beloved.
Continue with this *ghazal*, Oh good musician,
    keep up the meter, say it the same way,
    I crave this to go on forever.
O, Shams of Tabriz,
    the honorable Sun of Tabriz,
    rise from the East,
    I am the bird hoopoe,
    I crave the presence of Solomon.

HUSH DON'T SAY ANYTHING TO GOD

See my ashen face,
    feel my ceaseless pain,
    and don't say anything to God.
See my bleeding heart,
    my eyes flowing like a roaring river,
    all that you see, let it pass you by,
    and don't say anything to God.
Last night, your spirit came to the house of my heart,
    knocked on the door and said,
    come on, open up,
    and, hush, don't say anything.
I bit my hand when I saw you,
    I said, yearning for you is all too painful.
    He said, I belong only to you,
    let your hand drop
    and, hush, don't say anything.
He said, you are my *sornaa*,
    you can't cry without my lips touching you.
    Wait, for I will play you like a harp,
    until then, about the melody,
    don't say anything.

I said, stop dragging my soul all over the Earth.
    He said, any place I take you, come quickly,
    and, hush, don't say anything.
I said, how can you ask me to keep quiet,
    when I know you will invite me to dance
    amidst the flames,
    to let go and embrace the fire that is your Love,
    how can I not say anything?
He smiled like a rose in full bloom,
    he said, come into the heart of fire.
    There you will see
    what you thought was a flame,
    is only jasmine.
    What you thought was heat,
    is only a leaf on a tree.
    What you thought was a blinding glow,
    is only a bed of tulips,
    walk right in,
    and, hush, don't say anything.
Flames turned into a talking rose,
    the heat cradled me in its gentle arms,
    it said, except of the kindness,
    and generosity of the Beloved,
    don't say anything to God.

I SAW GOODNESS GETTING DRUNK

I am gone,
    lost any sense of wanting the wine
    of the nowhereness ask me,
    I don't know where I am.
At times I plunge
    to the bottom of the sea,
    at times, rise up
    like the Sun.
At times, the universe is pregnant by me,
    at times I give birth to it.
The milestone in my life
    is the nowhereness,
    I don't fit anywhere else.
This is me:
    a rogue and a drunkard,
    easy to spot
    in the tavern of Lovers.
    I am the one shouting *hey ha*.
They ask me why I don't
    behave myself.
    I say, when you
    reveal your true nature,
    then I will act my age.

Last night, I saw Goodness getting drunk.
    He growled and said,
    I am a nuisance, a nuisance.
A hundred souls cried out, but
    we are yours, we are yours, we are yours.
You are the light
    that spoke to Moses and said
    I am God, I am God, I am God.
I said Shams-e Tabrizi, who are you?
    He said, I am you, I am you, I am you.

DIDN'T I TELL YOU

Didn't I tell you
    not to go to that place?
    It is me, who is your intimate friend.
    In this imaginary plain of non-existence,
    I am your spring of eternal life.
Even if you lose yourself in wrath
    for a hundred thousand years,
    at the end you will discover,
    it is me, who is the culmination of your dreams.
Didn't I tell you
    not to be satisfied with the veil of this world?
    I am the master illusionist,
    it is me, who is the welcoming banner
    at the gate of your contentment.
Didn't I tell you?
    I am an ocean, you are a fish;
    do not go to the dry land,
    it is me, who is your comforting body of water.
Didn't I tell you
    not to fall in this trap like a blind bird?
    I am your wings, I am the strength in your wings,
    I am the wind keeping you in flight.

Didn't I tell you
    that they will kidnap you from the path?
    They will steal your warmth,
    and take your devotion away.
    I am your fire, I am your heartbeat,
    I am the life in your breath.
Didn't I tell you?
    They will accuse you of all the wrongdoings,
    they will call you ugly names,
    they will make you forget
    it is me, who is the source of your happiness.
Didn't I tell you?
    Wonder not, how your life will turn out,
    how you will ever get your world in order,
    it is me, who is your omnipresent creator.
If you are a guiding torch of the heart,
    know the path to that house.
    If you are a person of God, know this,
    it is me, who is the chief of the village of your life.

MY SPRING DIDN'T SHOW

Today my sweetheart didn't show,
    my heart-ravishing Lover didn't show.
That flower growing
    in the garden of my soul,
        tonight to my bedside didn't show.
Lost in the desert like an antelope,
    the scent of the musk of my gazelle didn't show.
Know this, my fervent musicians,
    the source of my passion didn't show.
Don't quiet down the *ney* and the *daf*,
    the one who quiets me down didn't show.
The *saaghi* of the soul didn't appear,
    the fix for my pain didn't show.
Shams of Tabriz, tell me a tale,
    for my season of Spring didn't show.

SECRETS OF THE DEATH OF LOVERS

Can you be killed more than once?
    Is there such a thing as death before dying?
We are our own worst enemy,
       but the Lover still wants to kill us.
       We have drowned in the ocean
       yet the waves still want to kill us.
We give our sweet life,
       freely, happily,
       because that king,
       with nectar and sugar cubes
       wants to kill us.
We eat, so we are ready and fat,
       we stand four-legged,
       and offer ourselves as the
       sacrificial lamb,
       because that darling butcher
       knows exactly how to kill us.
Like Ismail, put your neck on the
       dagger of Love
       with a smile.
       Don't pull back,
       as he comes for a kill.
The angel of death can not seize the Lovers,
       he has no hand in your destiny.
       The lovers of Love,
       are killed by Love and passion alone.
The public sees one thing,
       the Beloved does another.

The public sees
headless bodies on the ground,
as the Beloved
grants a hundred lives.
Try this:
detach your mind of this earth,
and then see
if the Beloved
will lift you up to the heavens
or if he will slay you instead.
The breath of the soul he takes,
comfort of the soul he gives,
the falcon of the soul he frees,
and the owl of sorrow he kills.
Christians believe this, others don't,
that Jesus put himself on the cross.
Remember Mansoor.
Every single Lover
will volunteer to die.
Do you know of others
who would do such a thing?
Should I stop here,
or should I reveal more of
the secret of the death of Lovers?
One last thought:
see how the non-believers die;
they die of violent deaths.
When Shams of Tabriz appeared
on the horizon like the Sun,
without any regard,
he killed the candle lights of the stars.

THE FIRE HAS ENGULFED YOU

Tell me who you are.
Your face is illuminating the
doorway to my heart.
Tell me who you are.
Waves of blood,
in every direction
night after night.
Tell me who you are.
The dead are dancing,
in their blossoming coffins.
It must be your life giving breath,
or is it the
second coming of Christ?
Tell me,
tell me who you are.
Carve a window in the
center of your chest.
Look inside,
look inside.
The fire has engulfed you,
and you
are not even aware.
See it now,
flames blazing through your chest,
like the presence of the Beloved.
They may seem like flames,
but they are
a purifying cup of my wine.

You are Jonah,
 captured in the body of a fish.
 Open up, open up,
 see now,
 your body
 is that fish.
Your body may be a holy robe,
 but if you want to
 become pure,
 lose this robe and
 gain the purity of your own heart.
You have drunk from this wine,
 but there is still some left.
 Go for another round,
 the real stuff is in the last sip.
If the Beloved
 places a sharp dagger
 on your neck.
 Sit toward death,
 for that is the way to die.
Know this,
 all the commands have broken.
 All the rules have crashed into each other,
 the future of justice is in danger.
 We are the revolutionaries,
 disrupters of order.
 We are a nuisance to judges.

If your passion
    will make you wait for tomorrow,
    slap him in his face,
    don't believe this hypocrite for a minute.
He doesn't sell you wine,
    he throws it to the
    wind.
    He will bend his back,
    but has no clue about bowing.
From the winter of passions,
    I have brought a
    body of snow,
    as per the request of kindness itself.
    Be careful, there are many meanings
    hidden in this riddle.
Oh, the honor of those from Tabriz,
    the Shams of Truth,
    pretension
    in your presence,
    in either of the
    two worlds,
    is a foolish game.

YOU WORRY TOO MUCH

Oh soul,
    you worry too much.
You say,
        I make you feel dizzy.
        Of a little headache then,
        why do you worry?
        You say, I am *your* antelope.
        Of seeing a lion here and there
        why do you worry?
Oh soul,
    you worry too much.
You say, I am your moon-faced beauty.
        Of the cycles of the moon and
        passing of the years,
        why do you worry?
        You say, I am your source of passion,
        I excite you.
        Of playing into the Devils hand,
        why do you worry?
Oh soul,
    you worry too much.
Look at yourself,
        what you have become.
        You are now a field of sugar canes,
        why show that sour face to me?

You have tamed the
winged horse of Love.
Of a death of a donkey,
why do you worry?
You say that I keep you warm inside.
Then why this cold sigh?
You have gone to the roof of heavens.
Of this world of dust, why do you worry?
Oh soul,
you worry too much.
Since you met me,
you have become a master singer,
and are now a skilled wrangler,
you can untangle any knot.
Of life's little leash
why do you worry?
Your arms are heavy
with treasures of all kinds.
About poverty,
why do you worry?
You are Joseph,
beautiful, strong,
steadfast in your belief,
all of Egypt has become drunk
because of you.
Of those who are blind to your beauty,
and deaf to your songs,
why do you worry?

Oh soul,
    you worry too much.
You say that your housemate is the
    Heart of Love,
    she is your best friend.
    You say that you are the heat of
    the oven of every Lover.
    You say that you are the servant of
    Ali's magical sword, *Zolfaghar*.
    Of any little dagger
    why do you still worry?
Oh soul,
    you worry too much.
You have seen your own strength.
    You have seen your own beauty.
    You have seen your golden wings.
    Of anything less,
    why do you worry?
You are in truth
    the soul, of the soul, of the soul.
    You are the security,
    the shelter of the spirit of Lovers.
    Oh the sultan of sultans,
    of any other king,
    why do you worry?
Be silent, like a fish,
    and go into that pleasant sea.
    You are in deep waters now.
    Of life's blazing fire,
    why do you worry?

ONE STRAND AT A TIME

Once more,
  Love is pouring down my ceiling
  and my walls.
Once more,
    the lion of Love is revealing its
    deadly claws
    and my deer-like heart is thirsting for blood.
Once more, it's the night of the full moon,
    it is time for madness.
    All my immense knowledge
    cannot help me now.
Once more,
    Love has created another revolt in my body,
    and yet a new flame was placed in
    my heart.
The awakened sweetheart has rubbed my sleep away.
    Insomnia took my patience.
    Rain washed away my intellect.
    The Lover made me lose my profession.
    What good is my work anyway?
You wonder about the lineage of the Lovers,
    let me tell you about it.
Look at my Lover's hair,
    see those luminous strands,
    they are all in there,
    one strand at a time.

Once more, rise, rise, rise,
    resurrection time is here.
    Oh, the Beloved,
    bathe me in the essence of a
    hundred resurrections.
Like the way a garden burns
    in a hundred shades of orange in the fall,
    a Lover's heart shrivels for a sense
    of the Beloved's touch.
    Now the face of that charred garden
    is my field of flowers.
The garden of the world is burnt,
    but the garden of the heart is resurrected.
    The secret of that garden may be burnt,
    but the secret of the heart is resurrected.
The time of ecstasy has come,
    oh my prisoned body.
    The garb of health has arrived,
    oh my frail heart.
Look, two hundred Jupiters
    are dancing around my moon.
Oh the wise man of the ruins,
    how can I ever repay this?
    Give away my
    cloak, my garb and headdress.
    What value can these have
    when the soul of the universe
    is but a gulp for my drunken sweetheart?

My Love business is booming,
    but don't credit the consultants.
    I am done with the consultants
    and the pundits,
    they call you *Jafar* the imposter.
Little do they know,
    that you are my Shams the Flyer.

AWAKEN THE DRUNKS

Awaken the drunks
    from the sea of wine.
    Awaken the drunks,
    like a soul is awakened
    by the Beloved.
Oh the bringer of wine,
    and the bestower of eternal life,
    bring my next sip from that ancient barrel.
Make your soul like a huge vessel,
    to hold the wine of the Beloved.
Look at that friend,
    he knows this wine
    is not taken through the mouth,
    but still he is sticking his tongue out.
Oh *Saaqhi*, pour me the wine,
    pour it from your eyes to my eyes.
    Pour it so even the mouth
    won't know anything of it.
When a letter of my Beloved arrived,
    I bowed to his eloquence.
    Oh Shams, your each word
    scatters pearls across the field.

GO BACK TO SLEEP

Go back to sleep.
    Yes, you are allowed.
You have no Love in your heart,
    go back to sleep.
His Love and his sorrow
    are exclusive to us,
    you go back to sleep.
I have been burnt
    by the sun of the sorrow of Love.
    You have no such yearning in your heart,
    go back to sleep.
The path of Love,
    has seventy-two folds and countless facets.
    Your love and religion
    is all about deceit and hypocrisy,
    go back to sleep.
We put ourselves in Love's hands,
    and will wait for her bidding,
    since you are in your own hands,
    you can go back to sleep.
I consume nothing but pain and blood,
    and you, the finest delicacies;
    and of course after each feast,
    you may want to take a nap.
    So just go back to sleep.
I have torn to pieces my robe of speech,
    and have let go of the desire to converse.
    You who are not naked yet,
    go back to sleep.

INTELLECT SAYS, LOVE KNOWS

Let me tell you what Love feels like.
You are walking through a fall,
    it consists of blood,
    it is more like a curtain of blood.
    You struggle your way through it.
    You shut your eyes at times,
    you close your mouth and hold your breath.
Finally when you reach the other side,
    you see a field of flowers,
    you hear birds chirping,
    a cool breeze is playing with your hair,
    you feel the wings of the butterflies
    brushing against you.
That garden, my friend, is
    Love.
So now you know
    why we say,
    "for those who seek Love,
    there is much work to be done."
I laughed when I heard the Intellect say:
    "there are only six directions,
    and beyond them there is nothing.
    That is the limit,
    there is no place beyond what we see."
Love says:
    "Oh, my friend,
    there is a place,
    and I have gone there many times."
The Intellect saw a bazaar and

began trading right away.
Love saw the same bazaar and
    saw a hundred more
    amazing places beyond that.
Remember Mansoor,
    he trusted the essence of Love,
    he went on the pulpit
    proclaiming his love for Love.
Yet the people of the mind still crucified him.
The Lovers may seem to be in much pain,
    but inwardly, there are celebrating.
    The dark-hearted people of the mind,
    inwardly, are in much denial.
The Intellect says:
    "don't take another step toward
    annihilation,
    it's nothing but thorns."
Love says to the Intellect,
    all those thorns are
    within you.
Be silent,
    and pull the thorn of living
    out of the foot of the heart,
    until you can see,
    in your inside,
    that field of flowers.
Shams of Tabriz,
    you are like the Sun,
    for the cloud of speech.
When you rise,
    your countenance
    evaporates all dialogue.

I HAVE COME TO SHINE

I have come
    to pull you by your ear,
    and bring you to myself.
    I will make you selfless,
    I will make you fearless,
    then I will place you in the
    heart and the soul of the king of Souls.
I have come like a breeze of Spring
    to you, oh, field of flowers,
    so I can keep you by my side,
    and hold you tight.
I have come to shine on you,
    as you walk this path.
Like the prayer of lovers,
    I will help you reach the
    roof of the heavens.
I have come to take back that kiss
    that you stole from me.
You are my catch, my game,
    my prey, my hunt.
You have escaped my trap so far,
    but run toward that trap once again.
    Run, run, or I will chase you there.
Remember what the lion said to the deer.
    "You are so beautiful,
    you are so lovely
    run in front of me,

so I can catch you
and tear you to pieces."
Be like the deer, accept the wounds
like a shield of a warrior.
Don't listen to anything
but the whooshing of the arrows heading
toward you.
From the dust of the Earth to a human being,
there are a thousand steps.
I have been with you through these steps,
I have held your hand and walked by your side.
You may think that I have left you
on the side of the road.
Don't complain,
don't become mad,
and don't open the lid of the pot.
Boil happily and be patient.
Remember what you are being prepared for.
You are a lion's cub,
hidden inside a deer's body,
with one strike I will wipe that illusion
and rid you of it.
You are my ball, and you roll because
of the strike of my polo mallet.
Just remember,
it is me who is chasing you
even though it is me who is helping you run.

IF YOUR HEART IS NOT WITH ME

If your heart is not with me,
    sitting together is not enough.
If your mouth is closed, but your heart is on fire,
    bathing in a stream is not enough.
If in the body there is no soul,
    the face lacks the spark.
    If there is no food on the table,
    having silver trays is not enough.
If you fill the earth to the sky,
    with amber and musk,
    if you have not a spiritual guide,
    all that perfume is not enough.
If you escape the fire,
    you will be sour and raw,
    like a dough.
Choosing a hundred lovers and sweethearts
    is not enough.

CRADLE MY HEART

Last night,
    I was lying on the rooftop,
    thinking of you.
    I saw a special Star,
    and summoned her to take you a message.
I prostrated myself to the Star
    and asked her to take my prostration
    to that Sun of Tabriz.
    So that with his light, he can turn
    my dark stones into gold.
I opened my chest and showed her my scars,
    I told her to bring me news
    of my bloodthirsty Lover.
As I waited,
    I paced back and forth,
    until the child of my heart became quiet.
    The child slept, as if I were rocking his cradle.
Oh Beloved, give milk to the infant of the heart,
    and don't hold us from our turning.
    You have cared for hundreds,
    don't let it stop with me now.
At the end, the town of unity is the place for the heart.
    Why do you keep this bewildered heart
    in the town of dissolution?
I have gone speechless, but to rid myself
    of this dry mood,
    oh Saaqhi, pass the narcissus of the wine.

HOW SWEET IS SELFLESSNESS

No matter where you are.
No matter what the circumstance of your life,
 be it like sugar or
 be it like poison,
 how sweet is selflessness.
If you are looking to get ahead,
 and you don't seem to succeed,
 how sweet is selflessness.
If you fall in his trap,
 and drink his soul wine.
 When you try to come out and
 don't find the secret hatch,
 how sweet is selflessness.
Don't be afraid,
 you still have time
 you haven't died yet.
Hurry up,
 you almost have no time,
 you haven't died yet.
 Give up that gold and receive a tender body,
 how sweet is selflessness.
Why are you so cold?
 Is it snowing in you,
 dissolve that to become great.

The life's little sorrows
you take too seriously.
How sweet is selflessness.
Don't think that you are in a trap.
My cup is full of wonders.
At this old age,
think of a new life,
how sweet is selflessness.
Why are you still sober,
can't you see this ocean of wine?
Don't tell me
now you want to become religious.
How sweet is selflessness
Oh Beloved, meet us in the garden,
sit in the middle of the gathering of the drunkards.
There is a cup in everyone's hand,
how sweet is selflessness.
Behold this King,
who watches all the souls.
Enter his land and,
emerge from the other side
victorious.
How sweet is selflessness.

BECOME A MIRROR

Oh candle of the world,
    your light did not brighten our circle,
    where were you last night?
Be honest,
    where did you hide that
    luminous face?
Please look in my direction,
    can't you see my heart
    thirsting for you?
    Perhaps you have found
    another treasure to look after,
    another mirror to unwrap your beauty to.
Last night,
    I searched for you until dawn,
    weeping and sobbing, looking everywhere.
    Today my heart is not with me,
    it must be in the mosque,
    saying prayers for your safe return.
Oh Love,
    you are a shadow of a brilliant light,
    and this world is *your* shadow.
    I am your shadow.
    Who has ever seen light
    be separated from its shadow?

At times,
the shadow is moving by its side,
at times, it vanishes inside the light.
Look,
God is walking by your side
and lost in him is all the light.
It is shadow's turn to shine.
It is shadow's turn to shine.
The shadow
is extracting light.
It is pulling God's light to become bright.
The Lover and the Beloved
are like a mirror for each other,
one is the cause for the other's effect.
Unless you become that mirror
we can't call you a Lover.

LOVER ME

Lover me, cave me,
    the sweet burn of Love me.
Lover you, cave you,
    Shams protect me.
Noah you, soul you,
    conqueror and the conquered you
    the awakened heart you.
    Why hold me at the gate of your secret?
Light you, celebration you,
    the victorious land you
    the bird of Mount Sinai you.
    You carry me on your tired beak.
Drop you, ocean you,
    compassion and rage you,
    sugar you, poison you.
    Please don't continue to hurt me.
The orb of the Sun you,
    the house of Venus you,
    the sliver of hope you.
    Open up the way for me.
Day you, night you,
    fasting you, the crumbs of a beggar you,
    water and a pitcher you.
    Quench my thirst, Beloved.
Bait you, trap you,
    wine you, cup you,
    baked and raw you.
    Please don't let me be unbaked.
If you don't run my body too hard,
    if you don't cut my way too much,
    if you try to help rather than
    make my life more difficult ...
Oh, all these words of mine.

DREAMS AND INITIATIONS

It has been nearly 10 years since my first translation of a Rumi poem. Throughout these years I have met many of you (whom I call *Rumi Lovers*) and have listened with excitement and fascination to your lovely and heartfelt stories of why Rumi means so much to you, or how Rumi has brought a positive transformation in your lives. I know some of your secrets too, like reading a Rumi poem every night before going to sleep, or carrying his translations in your purse so you can always have a poem handy. One woman actually suggested that my next book should be a paperback again, so it could fit in her purse easier.

I have always said that nothing takes you closer to Rumi than working with him directly, and I know many of you have taken my advise and are creating your own versions of Rumi based on my book *Rending the Veil*. I have listened with much joy as many of you recite them to me. I have heard your amazing dreams and experiences of Rumi and Shams as well. One dear friend mentioned that upon her first visit to the tomb of Shams, she heard Shams and Rumi's laughter within her own being. Another friend's initiation into the spiritual path was spearheaded by a dream of Shams (in the dream Shams' body was covered with that famous felt that we keep hearing about). Some of you have also shared your visions of Rumi with me. More than once have I heard you mention seeing the presence of Rumi in my performances. I am always deeply touched by your sharings.

I feel that "it is my turn now" (to paraphrase a Rumi poem) to share some of my experiences of Rumi with you. I have mentioned these only to a few close friends before, and I would like to share them with my larger circle of friends now. I have selected the following experiences out of many, mainly because of their importance and significance in my own process.

SHAMS' TOMB: The night before my very first recitation of Rumi, I had a vivid dream. In that dream I was visiting a tomb of a Sufi saint. I was there; I could see the plaques on the walls and was able to look around and take in the place. I had no idea who that saint was until a few months after, when I saw a picture of the inside of Shams' mausoleum. I realized then that I had visited the Shams' tomb in that dream. In Sufi tradition, seekers are often initiated through vivid dreams of the master's tomb. I felt very fortunate for the welcoming mat into Rumi's world.

INITIATION BY RUMI: A few years later, a night or two after I finished the manuscript for *Rending The Veil*, I had a dream where I found myself sitting in a cross legged position on a white sheep skin (that's what I use for my meditations). I looked around and noticed that I was sitting in a queue of an endless number of men. We were all in our thirties, and seated in cross legged positions on various types of cushions, blankets or animal skins depending on our tradition. I was the third person in line. We were in some kind of an outdoor monastery. I could see the walls surrounding the place on this bright beautiful day. I looked to my left, and a few yards in front of the line I saw a Sufi saint all dressed in white, even his sash was white. He had a long white beard. He looked elegant, regal and was extremely charismatic. He seemed to be about 6 feet tall. I was not shown above his lower lip. I immediately recognized him as Rumi. (It was later that I read in Nur Ali Elahi's book *Assar ul Hagh*, that he described Rumi as the Sheikh in White, because he appears to people wearing only white.) A moment later, he began walking toward us. Rumi walked by the first and the second person in line, and when it was my turn he swung this golden ball (the size of a billiard ball) which was attached to a golden chain which was connected to a ring on his finger (very similar to a yo-yo, but the chain was much shorter and the ball was a complete sphere). Rumi hit the ball on the top of my head, and I felt an immediate intoxication. He initiated me and moved on and I noticed that he only used his ball on a few other people. I felt very blessed to be initiated by him in such a magical ritual, and of course the timing of it could not have been more auspicious.

THE SWORD OF RUMI: A few days before one of my Rumi performances, I had a dream where I was faced with a column about five feet high and a foot in diameter, made of a stone that looked like marble but wasn't. I had a sword in my hand. My understanding was that this stone was impenetrable, and that nothing could cut through it. I knew that it was related to Rumi, and I didn't see it as an obstacle, but rather as a test of faith. I lifted up my sword and prepared to strike the top of the column. As I brought the sword down I yelled very loud, *"Yaa Hazrate Moulana"* (which is an invocation to Rumi in Persian). To my amazement the sword penetrated the column for about four inches and chipped the area of the contact. Needless to say I felt pleased with the outcome.

YOU ARE THE OWNER OF THE LAND OF LIFE: I saw one night in a dream that Shams' name and being was all of creation. He was the sky, the land, the clouds, the sun, and the air. I could almost see his name written on the particles of air and his eyes the size of the horizon gazing at me. I was immediately reminded of a line from Rumi in Persian where he says, "Oh, Shams, you are the owner of the land of life." Then I understood what Rumi meant when he said those words.

THIS SHAMS: Recently I had a dream where I saw an older man, sitting across a dinner table from me. There were many people dining at the table, mostly around my age, but they all seemed visually out of focus expect for this older man. I could see him vividly. He was bald and the white hair on the sides of his head had grown long to his shoulders. He was not attractive, and his face showed the passing of the years. He was clean- shaven and his eyes shone with wisdom. He looked at me, and said in poor English, "this Shams, this Shams." I woke up immediately, and all I could think of was how gracious and how compassionate it was of him to come to me in this way. I walked about all day in bliss, and found myself, saying to him in Persian *"shoma lot-fe-toon kheily ziyade"* (your compassion is great).

Having had the privilege and the good fortune of these visitations, it became clearer to me why the people of Konya acted so harshly toward Shams. In comparison with the grandeur of Rumi, Shams must have seemed like a vagabond, a sorcerer who had put a spell on their beloved Rumi. Konyians must have detested having a wild antisocial figure with no clear past, or a known family line come out of "nowhere" and steal their most important figure, their number one citizen. (Even the *amir* [ruler] of the region bowed to Rumi's superior intellect and charm and became one of his students.) I understand now why the only solution the people of Konya could come up with to "free" Rumi of this spell was to plot an assassination of Shams. (They burnt the witch so to speak.) It also makes much sense, why Rumi himself made sure that Shams' name is not forgotten. Rumi knew better than trusting the historians or even his sons and close disciples to the task of keeping the name of Shams alive. He took it upon himself and by naming the *Divan* after Shams and by using the Shams' signature in many of the poems he immortalized his beloved; and he cut off the bloody hands of the assassins from burying the memory of the one he cherished the most forever.

In 1991, after whirling for a few years, by chance I discovered a curious connection between they way I was whirling, and the way the Earth rotates and the solar system holds its proper order. I knew that all things in creation are in a state of perpetual whirling, from the sub-atomic particles to the galaxies—in another words, this is how the universe manifests itself. But then I realized that all things whirl/rotate/orbit/spin around an axis. This common thread is what my four-step method is about.

Just as the Earth turns around its axis, or the entire solar system orbits around the Sun, or a tornado spins around its eye, or the electrons circle around the protons, we can create an axis within our body to whirl around it (*fig.* 1). It takes only a few minutes to learn this method. The best thing about this method is that it works regardless of your age or your physical training, and just like yoga you can set your own pace. Of course those who are in better physical shape tend to do better. Although no quick lesson can take the place of actually training with the darvishes themselves, for those of you who are interested in whirling, but do not have the opportunity of training within an established whirling tradition, this is the next best thing. I have been fortunate enough to see some participants in my workshops who after a few tries have been able to whirl at an amazing pace with much comfort. I am happy to have discovered this quick method, and to be sharing it with you.

Why whirl? Whirling is an ancient form of centering and meditation. It has been used in many spiritual cultures throughout the world. Through whirling we harmonize with the energy of the creation, and form a more positive energy around us. Darvishes drop their black cloaks (a representative of their bodies) and begin to whirl as divine entities wearing all white. They believe that while they are whirling they are closest to being divine. We whirl counter clockwise to uplift the soul to the heavens. Some cultures (Buddhist in particular) tend to keep the option of whirling clockwise if they feel the need to bring a more earthly balance to their energy.

The following four-step method has been totally field-tested. This process is extremely easy. I have instructed many people in the past few years and have a high success rate. Before you begin make sure that:

- The ground you are whirling on is stable and level.
- You are not whirling on small rugs, blankets or mats that can move under you.
- You are not wearing shoes.
- You are wearing socks on smooth surfaces, or are barefooted on carpets.
- You are not wearing glasses.
- You have ample room to move about freely in your space, and keep a radius of 8 feet around you free of any obstacles.
- You are trying this on an empty stomach.

Figure 1:The Axis. *It was through a similar photograph of whirling that I discovered the axis.*

STEP ONE: Create an axis.

Everything in the universe is in a constant state of spinning and everything is perpetually turning around an axis. **By using our left foot, left leg, upper torso, shoulders, neck and head, we create that axis**. Please note that you are to make no additional movements or hold any special postures. Just stand in a comfortable natural erect posture and **be aware** that you have now created an axis, that is all (*fig. 2*). What is remaining of your body, which is your right leg and your arms will then turn around this axis. Please turn counter clockwise, and know that only one in every thousand tornadoes turn clockwise and the entire solar system (there are a couple of planets that are exceptions) including the Earth, rotate counter clockwise.

*Figure 2: Begin and end your whirl by standing
in a comfortable upright posture.*

STEP TWO: KEEP the ball of the left foot
in constant contact with the floor.

Just like a top that spins around a point, we will create this point by
turning around the ball of our left foot. Please note that this is not
Ballet and you do not need to actually turn around the ball of your
foot constantly. The entire process is highly organic and very nat-
ural in approach. Therefore, turn around the ball of your left foot as
you lower and lift your left heal to accommodate it. Your right leg
propels you forward as your left foot continues the turn. So as your
right leg pushes your body into the whirl, your left leg is on its heal
(*fig.* 3), and as your right leg finishes taking a step, your left leg turns
on its ball (*fig.* 4). Try this a few times on your own.

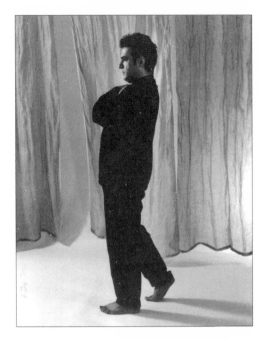

*Figure 3: As your right leg pushes your body
into the whirl, your left leg rests on its heal.*

Step Three: The eyes.

Keep the eyes in a comfortable, unfocused position. If you have dance training please do not "spot" (spotting will work against turning and you will not be able to whirl for long). Therefore try not to look at anything and maintain a blurry or unfocused vision. Let the images in the room pass you by without your visual participation. If you wear prescription glasses take them out before whirling. If you look at objects as you whirl, you will not be able to have a smooth turn, and you will be forced to stop your whirling after a few short tries. Please do not look at your hand either as you turn. Whirling is about freedom; we don't try to leave this cage of a body to fall into another cage of locking our gaze on our hands as we whirl.

Figure 4: *As your right leg finishes taking a step,*
your left leg turns on its ball.

STEP FOUR: HOW DO I STOP?

Just as you are about to come to a stop, pick a stationary object on the floor. It could be lint, it could be a chair, it could be a cushion, a pattern on a carpet, or a stain on a wooden floor. **Stop, stand comfortably (fig. 2) and lock your focus on that object**. Please do not remove your focus until the room has completely stopped turning around you. This step is most crucial to help you have a dizzy-free experience. Be patient and wait for the room to come to an absolute halt. Now you can feel free to move about. Congratulations, you have had your first whirling experience.

HERE ARE A FEW MORE POINTERS:

- When you start to turn, stretch your arms and keep your right palm up to the heavens and your left palm down to the earth. You receive the energy of the creation with your right palm and transmit the same energy with your left palm. This way you become a conduit for the transmission of the energy of the creation. You harmonize with the energy of the universe.

- Remember to breathe. Breathe, and be as comfortable as you can while whirling.

- Put on a music that you think is appropriate and has a steady beat (although music with a specific beat is not necessary, certain classical music or jazz will also do fine).

- Remember to keep your axis solid at all times, that is your pillar that you are turning around, so keep it steady, and please try not to be stiff.

- Enjoy yourself, and have fun with this. Just like Yoga, find your own pace and experiment with it as you go along.

As we say in in Persian *be-charkh* (you turn).
Have a great *charkh*!

A slight dizziness is normal after your first few tries, since your body needs time to get used to this new sensation. The author is neither responsible nor liable for any harm or injury that might occur to the participants for whatever reason by trying these exercises. Please try this at your own risk.

Ali: A Muslim saint and Prophet Mohammed's son in law. Many Persian mystics consider Ali to be the first Sufi.

Daf: A kind of frame drum.

Darvish: (Dervish) A Persian word for one who has renounced the world. Certain darvish orders of Iran trace their heritage back to the pre-Zoroastrian order of the *Mithra*. Their system of belief is based upon rigorous exercises, devotional movements, chants, proper diet, meditation, whirling, and non-attachment to the material proper-ties of the world. They also see a distinct difference between a darvish and a Sufi, although in many mystical orders of Islam the words darvish and Sufi are used interchangeably.

Forghan: An ancient Persian city used to be called the Asian Paradise. Currently in Turkmenistan.

Ghazal: A love poem, longer than 5 verses.

Ka'ba: The Muslim place of pilgrim-age. A cubed-shape shrine in the city of Mecca, Saudi Arabia.

Khezr: The immortal Green-Being, mentioned in the Koran. Some believe the vision of Khezr alone grants the seeker immortality.

Konya: (*Ghoniye* in Persian) A city in modern day Turkey, where Rumi spent the majority of his adult life. Konya also houses his shrine.

Mansoor: Mansoor Hallaj also known as Mansoor Mastaane. A 10th Century Sufi martyr. He was crucified for proclaiming these words: "*Anal Hagh*" (I am the truth).

Moulana: Our master. Rumi's title.

Ney: An end-blown bamboo flute. One of Rumi's favorite instruments.

Pir: Persian word for a spiritual master.

The Prophet: Muhammad, founder of Islam.

Rostam: A mythical hero. Created by the great Persian poet Ferdousi in his epic Shah-Naame.

Robaab: A kind of lute, Played in Afghanistan.

Rumi: His full name is Moulana Jalaluddin Mohammad Ebne Sheikh Bahauddin Mohammad Ebne Housseine Balkhi. The family name of Khatibi was also used by his father and grand father. Born in Persia, in the city of Balkh (in modern day Afghanistan) on September 30, 1207, and passed away in Konya (in today's Turkey) on December 17, 1273.

The Persians named him Rumi (the Roman) mainly because of the close proximity of Konya to the Byzantine Empire. Rumi was one of the most important figures of the Thirteenth Century, and has been called the greatest mystical poet of any age. Others have said that he can be compared in stature only to such Westerners as Dante and Shakespeare. He completed two epic collections of poems, each consisting of about 35,000 verses. The first is *Divan-e Shams-e Tabrizi* (the collective poems of Shams of Tabriz) which is a collection of passionate poems mainly addressed to God and to Shams as a vehicle for God's energy. The second is *Massnavi* (also spelled Mathnawi, his most famous work) which is a collection of guiding words for the students of mysticism. He is the national poet of these three countries, Iran, Afghanistan and Turkey.

Saaghi: Cupbearer. In poetry of Rumi, Saaghi is the metaphor for the moment one is enraptured by divinely induced state of ecstasy. When one is experiencing this state, one says that the Saaghi has brought the wine of love.

Samaa: In poetry of Rumi Samaa refers to the whirling dance of the Darvishes. This sacred movement is offered to, and symbolizes the constant movement of the universe. From the subatomic particles to the galaxies all are subject to rotation. Darvishes believe that the human body is no exception, and through whirling one harmonizes with the energy of the creation.

Sea of Oman: The Eastern section of Persian Gulf that flows into the Indian Ocean.

Shams of Tabriz: His full name is Shamsuddin Mohammad Ebne Ali Ebne Molkdaad. Rumi's spiritual friend who became the conduit for transformation for Rumi, and because of this Rumi revered him. Shams also means the sun.

Sornaa: A wind instrument similar to Indian Shenai.

Sufi: The mystical branch of Islam, Sufism traces its origins to Prophet Mohammad and his son-in-law Imam Ali. Some Sufi orders consider Ali to be the first Sufi. In many spiritual orders of Islam the words Sufi and darvish are used interchangeably.

Two worlds: Here and hereafter. This world and the next.

Water of life: The inner nectar of immortality. The nectar that holds the essence of the creation. Described as a spring that one encounters in meditation.

Zolf: Hair. The state of being in the Beloved's presence has been described, as being caught in the Beloved's beautiful, net like hair. It can also mean illusion.

Beloved: God, perceived as one's closest friend, companion, and a lover. A universal mystical concept.

Breeze: The life-giving breath of the Beloved.

Burning: The pain that follows the process of spiritual growth and purification.

Desert: The universe, the plain of consciousness that needs to be crossed so one can attain self-realization.

Drunkenness: Being enraptured by the love of God. A divinely induced feeling of ecstasy.

Garden: A metaphor for a beautiful and a harmonious state of being. Also used literally as a flower field.

Hair: The state of being in the Beloved's presence has been described, as being caught in the Beloved's beautiful, net like hair. It can also mean illusion.

Killing: The destruction of one's ego, and its limited sense of identity. It especially refers to the breaking of one's attachment to the physical body.

King: God, the Beloved.

Nightingale: The soul singing to the Beloved.

Ocean: The universe, the plain of consciousness that needs to be crossed so one can attain self-realization.

Pearl: Represents maturation and compilation of ones character.

Rose: The eternal and perfect beauty of the Beloved. In Rumi's poetry the word thorn, is used as the opposite of rose.

Sea: The universe, the plain of consciousness that needs to be crossed for one to attain self-realization.

Sorrow: The pain of being away from one's loved one. In poetry of Rumi, the pain of separation from God.

Wedding Night: The night the soul (lover) joins in union with God (the Beloved). It also refers to the day a great saint leaves his body.

Wine: Nectar of love, divinely intoxicating presence of the beloved.

AUTHOR'S BIOGRAPHY

SHAHRAM SHIVA, born in Mashhad in the province of Khorasan in Iran, is known for his unique and passionate incantations of Rumi's poetry. Shiva is a major interpreter and performer of Rumi in the West, who speaks the language of Rumi and who has an unadulterated access to Rumi's original Persian poems. He has translated several hundred of Rumi's poems, which serve as the basis for his celebrated concerts and performances. His translations of Rumi have also been utilized by other current Western Rumi interpreters such as Andrew Harvey and Jonathan Star, and have appeared in educational textbooks and numerous other publications. His works include *Rending the Veil: Literal and Poetic Translations of Rumi* (Hohm Press, 1995), which was a finalist for the Benjamin Franklin Award and *A Garden Beyond Paradise: The Mystical Poetry of Rumi* (with J. Stars, Bantam Books, 1992). He is a longtime practitioner of Eastern mystical traditions. In addition Shiva has devised a new, four-step method in teaching the whirl, where he trains actors and dancers and conducts frequent workshops.